AF571946

CENSORED LETTERS

BETSY STRUTHERS

OAKVILLE NEW YORK LONDON

Canadian Cataloguing in Publication Data

Struthers, Betsy, 1951-
Censored letters

Poems.
ISBN 0-88962-250-7

I. Title.

PS8537.T78C46 1984 C811'54. C84-098746-3
PR9199.3.S77C46 1984

Published by Mosaic Press, P.O. Box 1032, Oakville, Ontario, L6J 5E9, Canada.

Published with the assistance of the Canada Council and the Ontario Arts Council.

Design by Doug Frank
Typeset by Speed River Graphics
Printed and bound in Canada

ISBN 0-88962-250-7 paper

Distributed in the United States by Flatiron Books, 175 Fifth Avenue, Suite 814, New York, N.Y. 10010, U.S.A.

Distributed in the U.K. by John Calder (Publishers) Ltd., 18 Brewer Street, London, W1R 4AS, England.

Distributed in New Zealand and Australia by Pilgrims South Press, P.O. Box 5101, Dunedin, New Zealand.

To my mother and father
who were both soldiers

and for Jim, always

CONTENTS

DECLARING WAR, 1914

In August, before school begins,
the children go mad with games.
Their screams invade my house
from the vacant lot next door
where the boys lined up in battle
aim long sticks for guns
and the girls, gathered under the apple tree,
play with an old doll and string.

But that play is a hanging. I see
the boys put down their weapons to join in,
one girl beginning to sing
in a voice as solemn as prayer
which stops when the doll is released to swing.
Glass eyes bulge from the china head,
cotton limbs jerk to the tug on the string.

Into the silent circle under the tree,
into the wasted field next door,
runs a boy who cries "War!" to his friends.
That afternoon, that summer, that life
falls and shatters, lies forgotten
as china shards among the roots
beneath the rotted leaves.

ROMANCE AND REALITY

Some things of course
cannot be made real

knights in shining armour
holy grails

you go to war
only because you need to

I know this

my staying here
is also my desire

*

To be heard
we need more
than telephones:
my lips
against your ear

Static on the line
collect long distance
from your camp in Kingston:
I could be talking
to Mars

I cannot commit
to the alien wire
the words I have made for you:
your name
as in a spell
coupled with my own

*

We make romance of this writing
this casual talk between lovers
as if it were morning
as if we were
still flushed with love

three letters a week
fifty-two weeks a year:
for how many years
of your lifetime
will you call this
the time of your life?

DEPARTURE SCENE IN BLACK & WHITE

As long as you can, you stand here with me, holding my
hand, watching your friends parade to the train
behind the flags and the bold tattoo of the drum
and bugle high school band. A man like any other, a teacher,
my husband distinguished in uniform. *A chap would be a fool*
not to go, if he gets the chance. I'd go for the change alone
if nothing else: the war will be over by Christmas.
An experience not to be missed. You hold my hand. Over there,
Paris is threatened, the taxis drive the gallants to the Front,
the chorus cancans to the beat of guns. *To have something*
clearly before you, that you know you must do, and can do,
and will do to the end of your strength. To escape your class,
the routine, endless days. To be one in a unit of men.
To be needed. I hold your hand. The train hoots at the marchers,
orders snap out loud above the cheers. You hug me then, you kiss
my mouth, my eyes, you stare for one long moment at our son.
And then, you turn. And then, you run. You wave your swagger
stick, your black boots cross the street in giant strides.
The hand I held salutes the khaki crowd. The man leaps up
the platform steps, turns once inside the door, and
disappears.

SONG

As we stood on the pier in Halifax harbour
watching your ship sail away, sail away.
God Save The King and raggedy cheers
echoed and boomed with the guns in the bay.

God Save The King we sang for a stranger;
cheers from the men along the ship's rail;
guns a salute and a pledge to protect us
who sang and who wept and who watched
while you sailed.

There were ladies in fur coats
and children with flowers,
fathers in bowlers and wives all alone.
All of us strangers and all now united
wanting you with us, wanting you home.

PRESERVING THE SELF

Not to imagine your eyes,
the pressure of your hand.
Not to dream the everyday desire.

Where you are now
men die
and beautiful boys
lie broken in the mud.

Tin soldiers, left out in the rain,
rust the colour of blood, blood
the colour of leaves
at autumn's ending.

I am too young
for this vision.
My own blood
follows the moon
swells and wanes
with the ordinary tides

that you, too, count
and swallow:
one more month apart
perhaps
one month closer.

THIS IS NOT DRAMA

this is history:
men go to war
and women wait
for years forgetting
not their own lives

across the deep silence
which is the ocean
across the echoing silence
which is the passage of time
across the silence which occurs
even during battle

words come to you
old songs, myths,
letters with ink
barely dry on the pages

this is still the same story
this is the snake
with its tail in its mouth

history: your ring
on my third finger
without a beginning
I pray
without an end

SLEEPING ALONE

The place where you should be
in my bed is invaded
by the black night and the cat's
purr and the pick
of her kneading paws.

The space where you should be
is in this hollow in the mattress
that I am too small to fill.
I clutch the pillow you slept on
yes, even to my breast,
and imagine I smell
your scent still upon it.

This night alone
the fear of the widow invades me.
You know how she purses
her thin dry lips;
how she sucks for pleasure
her bitten fingers;
how her legs stick together.

She is the cat's familiar.
She rides the wind that rattles that window.
She whispers to me her obscene secrets
in the night when I turn
to your place for comfort
and find this dark space
without you, empty as dreams.

THE HOME FIRES BURN

No bombs, no black-outs, no anti-
aircraft fire: your home,
I promise you, is peaceful.

Here is a picture of me
in volunteer uniform
in the canteen handing tea
to new recruits.

How I smile and smile
to hear their young male voices.
How I think desperately of you

when one hand touches mine
to light a cigarette;
when one glance follows mine
towards the door.

LOVE LETTER

If you should meet, on your next leave,
a woman who needs a man
gentle and knowing,

If she talks to you of the country
and listens to your tales of home,
If she takes you to her room
in a house smelling of bread and flowers,

If she strips quickly and leaves the lights burning,
If she holds you tightly to her for a long time
soaked also with your tears,

That will be my hand
that strokes your knotted spine,
my breasts you suck, my lips
that lull you into sleep at last

That love
is mine.

KNITTING THROUGH THE SOMME

On the first of July nineteen-sixteen,
on the first day of this long battle,
sixty thousand British soldiers
are shot going over the top.
A city of men destroyed;
a city of women, their children
never conceived.

I live, in this city of women,
old men and walking wounded,
a convent life, the day divided
by factory bells, by office hours.
The evening is the time of my temptation
when work is done, our son in bed,
your letters and the latest news
read once more. I wait then
to hear your step on the stairs,
to see you standing, proudly,
at the door.

To save myself from this despair
I do my bit. With hands that ache
for you, I knit the hours off
in rows of stocking stitch.
As though a simple sock could be a charm,
the needles' click the fingering
of a prayer. As though a scarf
would hold you in my arms
and bring you safely home
from over there.

HE SENDS HER A PICTURE OF HIMSELF, KNITTING

Now in the lull of battle
you learn to knit: gray socks,
a balaclava.

Purl and knit. Purl and knit.
Your mess-mates call you Granny.
They lounge around you posing
for a photo in the sun
on the stoop of a burned down barn.

Needles flash like sabres
in that sun, their gentle click
a mother's sound. Wool snakes
from the pack on the ground
around your bitten fingers,

fingers that I hold in my own
claws that ache in the grip
of the knitting. Purl and knit.
Purl and knit. Stitches dropped
not caught in time
keep the work
unravelling.

HAWKS AND DOVES

For three months now, no word:
you are either missing or dead.

So many are missing and dead,
the streets are full of black ribbons.

Blacks ribbons on the bonnets of widows
who hand white feathers to protesting men.

Men who eat no meat, who swear in clear voices
that honour is killing, that war is the rape of the sun.

Our own son plays at soldiers in the garden.
He punches a pillow and kicks at the enemy air.

Air fills with down that settles on his arms
in wings of white that weight him to this earth.

FROM FLANDERS FIELDS

In the beginning you write
that I should not imagine
the war. The reality,
you say, is mostly boring.
You march and move your camp
and march and move again.
Some days you sit in trenches
ducking bullets. Some nights
you crawl through stinking mud and wire
to shoot at other men
and curse the moon.

Then your letters become brief,
arrive less often. In them,
you damn the food, report
the weather, repeat the joke
that ghosts that year
are popular in France.
You say no bullet yet
has got your number.

After the last long silence
you send me only this copy
of a soldier's poem
about the dawn, about the singing
of small brown birds.

MOTHERING

Through dreams of carrion, a crow's insistent caw
wakes her to another morning. In spite of her husband
still sleeping beside her, she sees only torn flesh
in no man's land, hears only the beating
of ebony wings.

All my brothers are dead, their bodies lost,
unburied. She sees the crow with fingers
in its beak, she sees it glare and crook
its bloody claw at her.

I have become the mother to my mother.
I have become her comfort in the dawn
when she comes to me with photographs and tears.
In my embrace, she rocks and nods,
her black hair frames her face in feathers,
her fingernails pick at the skin of her arms.

HALLOWE'EN

Ghosts now appear openly,
walking down George Street at noon,
smoking cigarettes, laughing. I thought
I saw Roy Murphy and Bill Smith yesterday;
two strangers believe that I came after them
for more than news of you.

Bad things are happening in town.
Junger's shop window has been broken twice
though he's changed his name to Young
and says he's Swiss. The Taub's pet dachshund
Maxie has been lynched. "Death to the Hun"
was painted on the Weiss's fence.

The ghosts seep into the house
under the door with the draught.
They crowd around the fire, mutter
through lipless mouths
their words of horror

familiar as the bones in my knees that crack
when I rise to answer the doorbell's ring
and the children's chant.

TABLE TALK AT MADAME ANNATSKY'S

The parrot stalks to the end of its perch,
the clink of its chain ticking out time
the stopped clock on the mantel has forgotten.
Night closes in on the room, the table
circled by women, silent, holding hands.

Only the parrot's yellow eyes are open.
Also mine. I stare at the scarlet splash
its head makes against the wallpaper
faded and floral. The jungle stirs
in the widow's sitting-room.

Bird coughs. In my right hand
my mother's hand tenses and shakes.
She knows her sons will come. I'm here
I think only to support her. Fear
and hope whisper round the table.

Five women long for those who have Crossed Over.
Madame vows that someone's love will answer,
will tap the table legs, blow the candle out,
shake the hollow tambourine.
The women wait; the minutes stretch, uncounted.

The parrot may yet speak in the voice
of the newly killed. One of us
might recognize the dread familiar.
But nothing stirs the ring of hands
deserted first by soldiering sons,
now by the selfish dead.

LOSING FAITH

Spring, again, and the river
breaks through its ribs of ice.
Above the rush of water, ducks
in arrows squawk. A crow caws
twice, flaps down to peck
the detritus of snow. The birds
have come back, the robins and swallows.
You do not return.

From my window, I look down
on the birds that gather
by the river, on the lawn.
The bared earth is brown and barren
needing the tonic of rain,
the purge of green. No flowers
bloom. The mud cracks
in your garden.

My hand holds back the curtain
from the glass. A fist of cloth,
its knuckles white with bone
beneath red skin, its bitten nails
that dig into the palm, that try to cut
the lifeline, the loveline, the lines
that lie of luck
now you are gone.

NOT ENOUGH TEARS

How angry I am!
When all these tears
appear useless, shed for nothing,
shed for summer friends
whose sisters weep in my house
looking for comfort I couldn't give
for thoughts of you.

Listen, my brothers are gone,
your cousin Edward,
two of your colleagues,
almost thirty
of the local lads:
all dead
and you say
you had no time to write.

Do you never think of me?
I mourned you fifty times,
I prayed your name,
I told our son his father
was in heaven.

And you write to me of hell.
What greater hell than this
to live over and over,
your death?
I'd rather have your death
than your indifference.........

That's not true, that's not,
that's only anguish speaking.
I've cried so many tears
but never wept enough
to wash away the pity,
to drown my love in fear.

CAPTURING HIS IMAGE

Your sweater sleeves
are a little long on me
your pants are too tight
around my hips.
Dressed up as you,
I hug the faded wool on my arms
as though it were your skin
I could put on, your self
becoming me.

But your face eludes me now,
it wavers and fades.
I must believe
that we can both be saved
if I could picture
even in a dream
the way your eyes looked
that last time
they looked at me.

REMEMBERING THAT LAST SUMMER BEFORE THE WAR

Then, I could scarcely see you, for the sun
fills the bowl of the lake valley
with light keen as ice. The strain
of watching for you on the cliff
brings tears to my eyes and laughing
I dive again, rise to float
blind and content as drifting wood.

Alone, you climb the sentinel rock,
man shadow, wavering dot of black
against the granite blue. Arms raised to the sky,
you dive, you shatter the surface stillness,
pull me down into the silken deeps among the weeds
and, without words, with such need
I cling to you, your mouth impressed
on my naked lips.

SAND CASTLES

Even now, there must be summer
holidays, the return to the lake.
The lane to the cottage is rutted,
tufted with long grass and dog violets,
the door sticks and the screens
are rusted from much rain.

I don't go to the rocks now,
I don't dive. Toby paddles
in the shallows by the shore.
I lie on a towel under an umbrella
stuck in sand. Watching him.
A gull, black against the sun, plummets
after fish. It is all the memory
of that last summer, and you.

The flies this year are fierce.
Deer flies on this strip of beach
hum and hover. Bluebottles bask
on polished driftwood bones.
Green flies, midges, horse flies
struggle in spider webs, so many
webs strung between the reeds.
At night, black flies and mosquitoes
will rise and roast themselves
against the gaslight glare.

Right now, though, as I write this,
it is afternoon and Toby, four today,
makes a sandcastle. He dreams
you fight in armour on a horse.
He dreams your siege. He builds
inner defences, a watchtower tall
with slivers of stone. He plants
a seaweed flag, chants his own song
of heroes and victory.

In your last pencilled note to me, you wrote:
How fat the flies in France are, they have so much to feed on. I saw one crawling down a dead man's eye — surprising how these small sights are the most disgusting. The staff play at soldiers back behind Reserve, make a model of the Front, everything molded in mud, the trenches, pill-boxes, wire, the current shell holes and guns. A battle line is marked with scarlet thread, our men are tufts of blue and theirs are green. The officers stand round it, taking notes. A big show coming on. But, good news, a break from rain has come at last and I've got three days leave to find myself some sun.

Toby squats above his fort in silent dreams.
A deer fly crawls across the glittering wall
toward his hand. The lake, turned by the tide,
sends silver fingers creeping from the moat
to mine the gates of sand.

CASUALTY LISTS

There is so little news and what there is
is lies. I learn to read the signs:
the length of casualty lists, official
postcards from the front, the maps
of wavering lines. These foreign names
trip my tongue: Passchendaele,
Ypres. I whisper them
and wonder what they mean.

KILLED IN ACTION
WOUNDED
DIED OF WOUNDS
SHOT DOWN
GAS POISONING
ACCIDENTALLY KILLED
MISSING
MADE PRISONER
DROWNED

Names of the dead come to us
tardily in these close columns
of small black print
on the back pages of newspapers
bordered by ads for portable baths,
for sewing kits and soldier's comforts.

CENSORED LETTERS

What is left out
are vital details:
where you are
when you write me.

I think of your colonel in his tent
sifting through the thin blue pages,
his boredom, his pencil rips

space between words,
holes at the ends of the lines,
sentences cut and butchered.

Quite safe, you say, in blank
though blank has died
and blank
is what you wish me.

MARCHING SONGS

Walking by myself down a dusty road
in the country, late afternoon, September.
Humming to myself your songs: Tipperary;
Over hill, over dale; Mademoiselle from Armentieres.
Waving to the hawk that circles silently
so high in that clear blue that I cannot imagine
he sees me. Other birds are watching,
the swallows who seem to swoop after
their own business above the purple thorns
in the pasture and the chickadees that line
the elm tree branches, chattering in
their own tongue the gossip of the air.

A barbed wire fence
Something hanging there
A crow its wings stretched tight
its black head dangling free
Scarecrow
Its eyes pecked out
Flies
A rotten smell that seeps
above the scent of grass
Oh, it's a long way....
the caissons are rolling....
parlez-vous.... army in tears....

The corn here marches right up to the fence
(the kernels golden in their ordered rows).
A breeze rushes over the stalks, making me shiver,
making them rustle, drawing from their dry throats
the hoarsely whispered chant of tired men:

If you want to find the old battalion
I know where they are, I know where they are
If you want to find the old battalion
I know where they are
They're hanging on the old barbed wire
I've seen 'em, I've seen 'em
Hanging on the old barbed wire
I've seen 'em
Hanging on the old barbed wire

THE BULLET FACTORY

There is not one thing heroic about this work. To set free
a man to fight. To make the bombs that kill him. To fuse
the week in days of ten hour shifts. In the company of women
dressed the same, in overalls and cap, I rush the factory gate,
punch the clock, take my station on the line, wait for the whistled
order to strike on my machine. Bullets begin to come, presses
pound, files scream. Some of us scrape initials on the metal heads,
others engrave curses there, or prayers. Hands in shafts of sunlight
weave the strands of death. The stink of powder rises in the heat.

Why men would keep this from us, I fail to understand. A job
is no romance. Women lean from windows, smoking cigarettes on break;
women sleep in huddles on the lawn at noon. Last night, a smelter
oven blew, killed two girls, disfigured nine. Not my shift, thank
God. The foreman gives us half an hour to mourn; then the work,
the bloody work goes on.

KEEPING WARM

1

We work to keep warm.
Susan brings the wood in
from her farm
and Catherine and Carolyn
come up from the town
to add their labour.

A chain of women stands
between the cart and the woodshed
passing logs hand to hand.
Words steam in the cold air,
puff before our eyes
signals to the frost
lying undercover,
warnings to the ice.

2

Rain begins suddenly, mist
from a gun-metal sky
hardens to snow. Winter
we know as our intimate
enemy. We have tasted
his kiss on chapped lips,
his fingers pinch
at our own.

But all day we've worked
to deny him. Indoors
the woodstove simmers,
hot tea is ready to pour
in painted cups. Settled
in rocking chairs, feet
turned up to the fire,
we trade our small stories
and laughter.

While the wind
worries away at the chimney
and the wood
turns to ashes.

3

In the company of sisters, I face
the cold night down: ashes
are for gardens they insist.
The work demands its cycle:
Cut the tree, and chop it.
Haul the wood, and stack it.
Split the logs, and burn them.
Clean the ashes, save them,
spread them on the raw earth
in the spring.
                                        Circle of fire,
circle of faces bent over the table,
hands peeling apples, preparing
to preserve them.
Four women, together,
plan that garden,
the seeding and canning,
recall the necessary pause
between the labour
and the certain harvest.

SHELL SHOCK

The boy who lives next door has come home.
His mother is overjoyed, but anxious.
His father mutters of the honest wounds
of other men. I visit him in their garden
where he rocks on a kitchen chair,
his fists thrust into his armpits,
his eyes on the grass that grows, green
between his feet.

It is impossible for us to understand
this living in the cliche of horror.
He wasn't shot, he fell into a shell-hole,
lay there for three days, face down
in the burst belly of a German corpse.
When he was found, his mouth and his eyes
were open, his hands were crawling
also with its worms.

I sit with him in the garden. I speak,
he cannot hear. I write him notes,
he cannot answer. In that white noise
of bombardment, he is made to swallow
more than his own death. His eyes
and mouth sag open. A fly, unnoticed,
gently tracks the lines that crease
his apple cheeks.

THE ARTIFICE OF DESIRE

How I noticed from the first
he was different. Out of that mob of boys
who crowded our canteen, laughing loud
at jokes they must have thought we ladies
wouldn't understand (as though there could
be innocence, four years into war) his hand
touched my own.
                                        Not a boy,
a man. Who apologized and took his mug of tea,
and sat, and read a book. A thin book,
leather bound. And sighed and looked,
and caught me looking back at him.
How blue his eyes were then!
And I remember still
the shape his lips took
that first time he smiled.

*****

Will you laugh at the artifice of desire?
I invite three officers to tea: him, of course,
and two others, all married men. A civilized event.
He reads his poems, my sister sings, his friends
show Mother pictures of their wives
while Toby drives his train beneath the table,
tangles the couplings round our feet.

How I shiver in spite of the applewood
burning in the fire. How I chat and laugh
as though my fingers brush by chance
his thigh, when I reach to catch the boy.
As though his wrist by accident should rest
on Toby's cheek that lies against my breast
while he promises a story and kisses him goodnight.

*****

"Airplane!" Toby shouts and I know
it's him, even as the engine's roar
brings the neighbours running:
we've none of us seen a pilot
dare to fly so low before,
the wingtips kiss the treetops

as he passes.   He climbs
into that giddy blue and rolls
and spins and Toby, shrieking,
aims an imaginary gun.
Again he dives and comes
right for me where I stand
in the garden, my heart in my hands,
his shadow swallowing.
And this time I can clearly
see his face, his fist
as he throws me roses.
And then he's gone
leaves me here with open arms
dancing in the red
and scented rain.

*****

Then he comes unexpectedly one morning
when I'm baking bread, my face flushed
with the effort of kneading. I know
he's come to say good-bye, his unit posted
out to France at last. How ridiculous
to sit at opposite sides of the table,
the loaves rising between us, and talk
of my husband, his wife, of letters
and after the war.
There is no after the war.
Before it is too late, here
is my tongue that longs to taste
his flesh, my breasts aching
for those hands
that smooth and caress
the leather jacket of his book.
It is his gift for me.
That, and one kiss on my palm
as he takes his leave. A gentleman.
And me — I'd gladly sin
and sinning, swallow fate.

*****

Grief lies, in wait, a dragon
curled in on itself, brooding
over treasure: the portrait
in a silver frame, rose petals pressed
between the pages of a book.

Such a thin book, imprinted with
his name. The dragon stirs,
its sigh burns over me
as I read his poems again
scalded with slow tears.

*****

(Thanksgiving, 1918)

To lose faith now the war
is almost ended. They say again that Peace
will come by Christmas. What good
is peace to me, when he's been killed
and you no longer write?

His wife wrote to me
"because he said you were so kind
to him, before he left" and told me
all the details of his death,
an accident, a low dive on a dare.

She has the right to mourn,
to bear his name.
I have this guilty grief, this
despair, this worthless
angry pain.

SESTINA CELEBRATING THE PEACE

We, of course, didn't hear the crash of the guns' silence
or see the men pop, one by one, up out of the filthy earth
to cheer or anyway shake hands in that clear, bright air.
Here, peace came at six in the morning. Our taste for fire
exploded in stars over the townhall, the schoolbells ringing
like madness. Still, we were not in time with our tears.

But this morning was certainly not a time for tears.
No one was looking or wanting or needing a moment of silence
when we stood, as it were, with people all over the earth
singing our thanks for the peace into the frosty air
which shimmered with dawnlight and streetlight and fire
and shivered with all of us to the carillon's ringing.

If you could have seen us! The whole town was ringing
with shouts, bells, sirens and songs. Boys started a bonfire
down on the riverbank, danced crazy jigs on the bare earth
which clapped to the smack of their feet. Flags in the air,
strangers kissing the girls in their housecoats and tears
and nowhere, not even in church, a place to find silence.

Toby, roused by the noise, wanted to visit the fire
so we dressed in warm clothes and went out into that air
so keen I could smell the snow coming. What silence
the day could expect was broken by cheers, the ringing
of hands clapping in time to the anthems. And tears
were only a matter of feet frost-bound by the earth.

We stood with all of our neighbours there at the hearth,
our faces flushed by the thrill and the tongues of the fire
that licked the frost from our cheeks and the traces of tears
we scarcely noticed. With all that mad dancing and ringing,
the roar of the flames made their own brand of silence
that swallowed the fervour of every victorious air.

That morning, all the women in town wore such an air
even the widows seemed to forget their tears
and not one mother was seen with her hands wringing.
Although some of us, too soon, fell into silence
remembering the ones we've lost to the hungry earth
whose faces came to us singing out of the fire.

Such lost loved faces ringing the bloody earth,
that stain the clean air with their mocking tears
forged in a fire no passage of time can silence.

AT THE ELEVENTH HOUR

Cold fog smothers the embers of the fire
on the riverbank deserted now of revellers.
The bells have ceased. Nothing stirs
in the shrouded streets but a girl
hurrying home from the dairy.
The sky leaks a little, listless rain
that dulls the neighbours' many flags
to rags of bleeding dye.

The morning after has a tired taste,
victory's wine gone sour in the mind.
The eleventh hour of the eleventh day
of the eleventh month of this fourth long year
has come too late: numb with waiting
now I almost dread to hear your voice,
your coming home to such a wife
nullified by wasted time
and all the dear, dumb dead.

WHEN TOMMY COMES HOME AGAIN

In my dreams, it is always midnight, the station crowded
with wives whose bright dresses flare in the wavering light.
The train arrives an hour late. The soldiers lean from windows,
laughing leap down moving stairs. Couples clutch, they
kiss (I can imagine their tongues touch), couples rush off,
arm in arm, back home. The small thick groans of love
echo in the dark where I am left, still standing, all alone.

But, too soon, this: the platform is deserted but for me,
the white sun glares on sooty snow and pitiless bright rails.
The train comes in on time. One man descends,
not in uniform, leaning on a cane. My courage fails.
(You wear a moustache now, a thin gray streak outlines your
settled frown.) We stand, face to face. Still.
Our cold breath steams. We reach across the brittle space
at last, and couple hands.

THE LONGEST NIGHT OF THESE FOUR YEARS

We think it has been too long,
our separation. Ghosts
hug us from each other, invade
our bed. Not just these others,
that's an easy lie. I resent
those long, long lonely nights.
You hate me for these clean
and quiet sheets.

The moon swells on the silence
in our room, throws down
a blade of light
between us on the bed,
a cold sword, keen
and double-edged.

*****

Our bodies have not forgotten.
When we sleep
they turn into each other:
my back fits
your belly's curve,
your knees snug
into the crook of my own.

Through the dark hours
until the false dawn
disturbs us,
your hand
cradles my breast,
my heart
beats with blood
in your wrist.

*****

I wake to hear you weeping,
weeping; names bubble
from your lips as
all your friends
one by one
explode inside your head.

Still asleep, the tears distort
your face, replace the stranger
with the father
of my son, besieged
by the restless dead.

Not just with pity
but with arms of love,
I hold you from
the phantoms of your fears

And whether you hear
my murmured comfortings
or whether your nightmare
takes another course

Your muttered curses cease
in sobs that beg
(your head between my breasts)
for safety, for silence,
for home, for dreamless rest.

*****

In the hour after the moon sets and before the sun rises,
we lie in our separate darkness waiting for dawn,
silenced by the space of the years between us
which I cannot explain nor you describe.

What use to explain or describe when words make pictures
only the better to blind us? My hand
of its own volition strokes the scar on your chest,
your fingers trace the lines between my eyes.

And I remember the delicate thickness of your tongue
between my lips, and how the fine hairs of your shoulders
shiver under my caress. How my nipples swell when you brush
them with your own; how my thighs melt to meet your soft invasion.

There is no need for stories now my lips have found
your willing mouth. I suck on that one tongue that cannot lie,
that needs me, that saves me from drowning in the dark
of what-has-been, when what is past, has passed.

*****

Here are my desires
(I have just a few):
a new moon
a warm bed
long nights
with you

L'ENVOI, 1919

Go, my darlings, my chicks, my little ones.
I open the door and shoo you out into the rain
  on the long road to school, to work,
  to your inevitable wars.

Remember, the lark sings louder than the loudest
        bombardment,
      the grass grows green on the trenches,
        greenest over the graves.

If a sparrow should fall, broken by glass reflection,
        will it lie forgotten?
If a man should fall in the line of forward attack,
        will anyone notice?
If a woman should weave all day, every day, a pall of words
        will he pick it apart
        or wear it?

Go, my dear love, my precious heart.
Remember the time before irony invaded us
        when humours ruled
        and the goddess and the gods
        made sense

        and you swallowed my words
        your mouth on mine
        our tongues engaged
        in that first
        delicious battle

ACKNOWLEDGEMENTS

Some of these poems appeared in *event* and *Grain*.

Several have been broadcast on CJRT FM Radio's *Words and Music* programme.

Sources that suggested some of the material of these poems were: the letters of Eric and Donald Fowlds in the Trent University Archives; *Chronicles of Youth*, by Vera Brittain (Victor Gollancz, 1981); *But This Is Our War*, by Grace Morris Craig (University of Toronto Press, 1981); *Kathleen & Frank*, by Christopher Isherwood (Simon & Schuster, 1971); *No Man's Land*, by Eric J. Leed (Cambridge University Press, 1979); and *The Deluge*, by Arthur Marwick (Norton, 1970).